Table of C

1. <u>Yo Momma's so Ugly</u>
2. <u>Yo Momma's so Fat</u>
3. <u>Yo Momma's so Skinny</u>
4. <u>Yo Momma's so Dirty</u>
5. <u>Yo Momma's Breath Smells so Bad</u>
6. <u>Yo Momma's so Stupid</u>
7. <u>Yo Momma's so Old</u>
8. <u>Yo Momma's so Short</u>
9. <u>Yo Momma's so Cheap</u>

Yo Momma Jokes

THE CLOWN FACTORY

" Yo Momma So Fat……Even Dora Can't Explore Her"

1. Yo Momma's so Ugly

Yo momma's so ugly her own shadow's ashamed to be seen with her in public.

Yo momma's so ugly, when she looked in the mirror her reflection screamed in horror.

Yo momma's so ugly her birth certificate was a restraining order.

Yo momma's so ugly, when we went to a haunted house, she came out with a paycheck.

Yo momma's so ugly, when she was doing door-to-door sales, someone told her it wasn't Halloween yet.

Yo momma's so ugly, when she and your daddy go for walks they tell your daddy to put a leash on his dog.

Yo momma's so ugly, when we went to the zoo, a little boy pointed to her and said, "Daddy, can I feed that monkey a banana?"

Yo momma's so ugly, when she was born the doctor apologized for malpractice and gave her momma a refund.

Yo momma's so ugly people give her dog treats at the pet store.

Yo momma's so ugly the last time I saw something that looked like her, I pinned a tail on it.

2. Yo Momma's so Fat

Yo momma's so fat she hopped in an elevator to go up and it went down.

Yo momma's so fat she makes a monster truck a low rider.

Yo momma's so fat she goes to a restaurant, looks at the menu, and says, "Okay!"

Yo momma's so fat she sank the Titanic.

Yo momma's so fat I had to take a train and two buses just to get on her good side.

Yo momma's so fat she has to iron her pants on the driveway.

Yo momma's so fat, when we went to a kid's birthday party, everyone thought she was the bounce house.

Yo momma's so fat, she went to Red Lobster for endless shrimp last month and she's still there.

Yo momma's so fat, when she walks down the street, they have to redirect traffic.

Yo momma's so fat her belly button has an echo.

Yo momma's so fat she dislocated her shoulder trying to scratch her back.

Yo momma's so fat your daddy gave her a spare tire as an engagement ring.

3. Yo Momma's so Skinny

Yo momma's so skinny, when I locked myself out of my apartment, she slipped under the door and let me in.

Yo momma's so skinny a thong bikini looks baggy on her.

Yo momma's so skinny she turned sideways and disappeared.

Yo momma's so skinny, if she had dreads I'd grab her by the ankles and use her to mop the floor.

Yo momma's so skinny she uses Chapstick for deodorant.

Yo momma's so skinny people in Ethiopia are collecting donations for her.

Yo momma's so skinny I can blindfold her with dental floss.

Yo momma's so skinny she can hula hoop in a Fruit Loop.

Yo momma's so skinny when she wore a yellow dress she looked like a No. 2 pencil.

Yo momma's so skinny she was the understudy for the tree in *Merry Christmas, Charlie Brown*.

Yo momma's so skinny everyone thought she was the coat rack at your birthday party.

Yo momma's so skinny she fell through the cracks on the sidewalk.

Yo momma's so skinny your daddy uses her as a toothpick.

4. Yo Momma's so Dirty

Yo momma's so dirty homeless people throw change at her when she sits on a park bench.

Yo momma's so dirty, when she told your daddy to take out the trash, he put her out on the curb.

Yo momma's so dirty, when I called her on the phone I got an ear infection.

Yo momma's so dirty when she shook her hair out, your little sister yelled, "Oh look, it's snowing!"

Yo momma's so dirty, when her momma threw her out on the street she got a fine for littering.

Yo momma's so dirty she turned Snow White black.

Yo momma's so dirty her elbows leave skid marks on the dinner table.

Yo momma's so dirty she stains your daddy's clothes when they hug each other.

Yo momma's so dirty she leaves a ring around the public swimming pool.

Yo momma's so dirty she went to the car wash and still couldn't get clean.

Yo momma's so dirty she swam in the lake and all of the fish died.

5. Yo Momma's Breath Smells so Bad

Yo momma's breath smells so bad, when she starts talking, the sewer rats ask each other what's that nasty smell.

Yo momma's breath smells so bad that skunks hold their nose when she breathes out.

Yo momma's breath smells so bad her teeth didn't fall out, they ran away.

Yo momma's breath smells so bad her dentist has to wear a gasmask.

Yo momma's breath smells so bad I don't know if I should give her a Tic Tac or a piece of toilet paper.

Yo momma's breath smells so bad she makes onions cry.

Yo momma's breath smells so bad the dog won't even lick her face.

Yo momma's breath smells so bad, when she exhales her eyes tear up.

Yo momma's breath smells so bad, when she stuck her tongue out it was on a stretcher.

Yo momma's breath smells so bad, it's considered a weapon of mass destruction.

6. Yo Momma's so Stupid

Yo momma's so stupid, when I was drowning and yelled for a life saver she asked, "Cherry or grape?"

Yo momma's so stupid she thought menopause was a button on the VCR.

Yo momma's so stupid she put a peephole in a glass door.

Yo momma's so stupid she asked me what kind of jeans I had on. I said, "Guess," so she said, "Levi's."

Yo momma's so stupid, when I told her to butt out, she dropped her pants.

Yo momma's so stupid, when she saw the Exit sign above the door, she immediately left the building.

Yo momma's so stupid, when I asked her if she was good at

spelling, she told me she didn't know magic.

Yo momma's so stupid, when I told her I had chicken pox, she asked me if they were grilled or crispy.

Yo mama is so stupid that when she took you to the airport and a sign said "Airport Left," she turned around and went home.

Yo momma's so stupid she put a quarter in a parking meter and waited for a gumball to come out.

Yo momma's so stupid she went out to the garden with a measuring spoon when the recipe called for two cups of flour.

Yo mama is so stupid that when she went to take the 44 bus, she took the 22 twice instead.

Yo momma's so stupid, when they told her she had to repeat

eighth grade, she said, "Eighth grade."

7. Yo Momma's so Old

Yo momma's so old, after I bought candles for her birthday, the store didn't have anymore in stock, so I had to go to another store to get some more, and then another one after that, and I still don't have enough for her damn cake!

Yo momma's so old she knew Mr. Clean when he had dreadlocks.

Yo momma's so old, when God said, "Let there be light," she flipped the switch.

Yo momma's so old, when she was in school there was no history class.

Yo momma's so old she used to play in the sandbox with George Washington.

Yo momma's so old she remembers Abraham Lincoln as a baby.

Yo momma's so old the fire department came when we lit the candles on her birthday cake.

Yo momma's so old the date on her birth certificate says B.C.

Yo momma's so old she used to hitch a ride to work with Fred Flintstone.

Yo momma's so old she named the Nina, the Pinta, and the Santa Maria.

Yo mommas so old her first baby picture is carved in a cave somewhere.

8. Yo Momma's so Short

Yo momma's so short she has to use a ladder to get up on the curb.

Yo momma's so short she has to stand on her tippy toes to drink out of a straw.

Yo momma's so short, when I dissed her, she tried to jump kick me in the ankle.

Yo momma's so short she broke her leg trying to get off the toilet.

Yo momma's so short she goes mountain climbing on ant hills.

Yo momma's so short she tripped over a thimble.

Yo momma's so short, when she told your daddy she wanted to live in a bigger place, he moved her into Barbie's Dream House.

Yo momma's so short her above ground pool is a cereal bowl.

Yo momma's so short she uses a washcloth as a beach blanket.

Yo momma's so short she has to get a running start to jump in bed.

Yo momma's so short she has to drive a matchbox car.

Yo momma's so short she goes figure skating on an ice cube.

9. Yo Momma's so Cheap

Yo momma's so cheap, when you spit, she yells at you for wasting water.

Yo momma's so cheap she only showers when it's raining.

Yo momma's so cheap, for your first birthday, she put a bunch of stuffed animals in the backyard and said you were at the zoo.

Yo momma's so cheap she demanded a refund at the dollar store.

Yo momma's so cheap, for Halloween she threw a pillowcase over your head and called it a costume.

Yo momma's so cheap she let her hair fall out to save on haircuts.

Yo momma's so cheap she tried to use coupons at a yard sale.

Yo momma's so cheap she refuses to pay attention.

Yo momma's so cheap she goes to the mall food court and hides free samples in her cheeks. Then she spits them out on a plate and says, "There's your dinner."

Yo momma's so cheap she collects cereal box prizes and gives them to you on Christmas.

Yo momma's so cheap she uses plastic bags as luggage.

Rolling on the floor with laughter? If so, check out other CLOWN FACTORY titles.

Even More Yo Momma Jokes!

Autocorrect Fails!

Blonde Jokes

INSULTS

Ginger/RedheadJokes

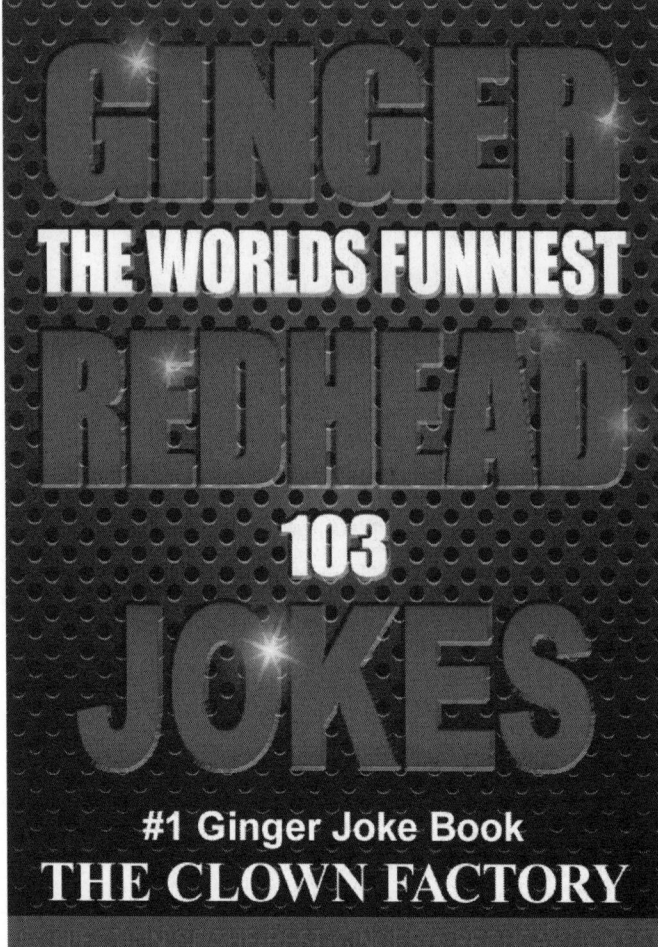

Hilarious Pickup Lines

Sports Jokes

THE WORLDS FUNNIEST SPORTS 103 JOKES

#1 Sports Joke Book
THE CLOWN FACTORY
COLLECTION OF THE BEST SPORTS JOKES EVER!